The World's Greatest Collection of

Rib-Ticklin'

RIDDLES

The World's Greatest Collection of
Rib-Ticklin'
RIDDLES

BARBOUR
PUBLISHING

Riddles are taken from *Lots O' Riddles* by Carrie Brown, published by Barbour Publishing, Inc.

Published by Barbour Publishing, Inc., P.O. Box 719, Uhrichsville, Ohio 44683 www.barbourbooks.com

Our mission is to publish and distribute inspirational products offering exceptional value and biblical encouragement to the masses.

 Member of the
Evangelical Christian
Publishers Association

Printed in the United States of America.
5 4 3 2 1

Contents

All in a Day's Work

Why did the carpenter quit his job?
He was board.

Why are carpenters in charge
of building contracts?
*They like to hammer
out all the details.*

How did the carpenter use only one
brick to finish building a house?
It was the last one.

What kind of music do cobblers listen to?
Sole music.

What is the rank of a Marine dentist?
Drill Sergeant.

What is the fastest way
to annoy a doctor?
Take away his patients.

What kind of music do
steel workers love?
Heavy metal.

Why did the pop star smack *The Guinness
Book of World Records* repeatedly with a hammer?
She wanted to produce a hit record.

What's black and white, black
and white, black and white?
A waiter rolling down the stairs!

If a gardener has a green thumb and
bankers have gold thumbs, who
has a black-and-blue thumb?
A carpenter.

Why did the banker sign
up for an art class?
He liked to draw interest.

What piece of jewelry do
boxers always wear?
A ring.

What kind of people make
the best grave diggers?
*Excavators who take their
job very seriously.*

Who is in charge of keeping
the railroad running?
The track coach.

Why was the car mechanic fired?
He took too many brakes.

How can you tell if the minister
is working on his sermon?
See if he is practicing what he preaches.

What did the surgeon say to his patient when he
finished the operation?
"That's enough out of you."

How did the carpenter break his teeth?
He chewed his nails.

Why are magicians given hazard pay?
*They have to pull their hare
out at every show.*

If Mr. Green sells cupcakes in his grocery
store for 39 cents each, how should he
price upside-down cakes?
They should be 63 cents each.

Who is the first person in an
orchestra to be hit by lightning?
The conductor.

How did the salesman call his client?
He used his sell phone.

Animal Kingdom

What animal is impossible to
carry on a conversation with?
A goat—he always wants to butt in!

What animal has more lives than a cat?
A frog. He croaks every night!

Why can't you play a joke on a snake?
Because you can't pull their legs!

What animal isn't born with wings,
but has the innate ability to fly?
*A caterpillar isn't born with wings,
but it will fly when it becomes a butterfly.*

What does a frog do when
his eyesight goes bad?
Goes to the hoptician.

Why does the giraffe have
such a long neck?
*Because its head is so
far from its body.*

Why did the otter cross the road?
To get to the otter side.

What do you say when you see
a snail drive past you in a car?
"Look at that escar-got!"

Why is it hard for teenage
turtles to be rebellious?
They can never run away from home.

What vegetable do you get when
an elephant walks through your garden?
Squash!

What's black and white, black and
white, black and white, and green?
Three zebras fighting with a pickle.

What did the teddy bear say
when he was offered dessert?
"No thanks, I'm stuffed."

What kept the performing
pony from singing?
It was a little horse.

What does a skunk use
to defend itself?
In-stinks.

Why did the weasel cross the road twice?
He was a double-crosser.

What has four eyes, one tail,
six legs, and two heads?
A person on horseback.

What did the toad say after
listening to one of the rabbit's jokes?
 "You croak me up!"

What animal rows quickly with
four oars but never travels
beyond his front door?
 A turtle.

Why are gophers so busy?
*They always have to go-pher
this and go-pher that.*

What kind of turtle always
has a bad attitude?
 A snapping turtle.

What do you call a sick alligator?
 An illigator.

What do you call a one-
hundred-year-old ant?
 An antique.

What kind of ant is good at math?
An account-ant.

Where do polar bears like to vacation?
Brrr-muda.

What do you get if you cross a
snowman with an alligator?
Frostbite.

What do you call a grizzly
bear with no teeth?
A gummy bear.

How do bears walk around?
With bear feet.

How does a skunk's car run?
On fumes.

What wears a coat all winter
and pants in the summer?
A dog.

What happens when a frog's
car breaks down?
He gets toad away.

What do you call a group
of mice in disguise?
A mousequerade party.

Where do worms like to
go for dinner?
Anywhere that is dirt cheap.

Why won't banks allow
kangaroos to open accounts?
Their checks always bounce.

What has twelve legs, six eyes,
three tails, and cannot see?
Three blind mice.

How do you keep a skunk
from smelling?
Hold its nose.

What animal is the strongest?
A snail. He carries his house.

Where does a skunk sit in church?
In a pew.

What do you call two spiders
that just married?
Newlywebs.

What do you get when you cross
a rabbit and the World Wide Web?
A hare Net.

What do you get if you
cross a parrot with a cat?
A carrot.

What is as big as a hippopotamus,
but weighs nothing at all?
The hippo's shadow.

What has keys but can't open locks?
Monkeys, turkeys, and donkeys.

How did the zookeeper
catch the escaped cat?
The leopard was spotted.

What dangerous animal did
Mrs. Washer have in her backyard?
A clothes lion.

What kind of snake is
good at math?
An adder.

What is black and white
and red all over?
A blushing zebra.

Brainteasers & Mindstumpers

Little Tommy suddenly found himself surrounded by thirty galloping horses, twenty-five charging bears, and ten roaring lions. How did he survive this situation?

He got off the carousel.

Four cars come to a four-way stop, each coming from either North, South, East, or West. It isn't clear who arrived first, so they all go at the same time. No one crashes, but all four cars successfully continue on their way. How is this possible?

They all made right-hand turns.

An archaeologist found a coin dated 62 BC and immediately declared it a fraud. How did he know it wasn't real?

BC stands for "Before Christ." This dating system wasn't used until after Christ had been born.

Maggie woke up one day with a toothache and went to the only dental practice in town to have it fixed. The dental practice had two partners, Dr. Smith and Dr. Jones. Dr. Smith has a beautiful smile, while Dr. Jones has a mouth of ugly, crooked teeth. Who should Maggie see about the toothache?

Dr. Jones. Since it is the only dental practice in town, Dr. Jones must fix Dr. Smith's teeth and vice versa.

A boat has a ladder that has six rungs. Each rung is one foot apart. The bottom rung is one foot from the water. The tide rises at twelve inches every fifteen minutes. High tide peaks in one hour. When the tide is at its highest, how many rungs are under water?

None. The boat rises with the tide.

Melissa was out shopping one day. She met her father-in-law's only son's mother-in-law. What did Melissa call her?

She called her "Mom."

If a farmer has five haystacks in one field and four haystacks in the other field, how many haystacks would he have if he combined them all in the center field?

One. If he combined them all, they would become one big haystack.

A woman drove to the video store. She got out, and accidentally locked her keys in the car. She went into the store to rent some videos. She came back out and unlocked the door without touching "anything" on the outside of the car. How did she do it?

The car was a convertible and she reached inside to open the door.

Marco and Anna were sitting in their living room one night. While Marco was watching television, Anna was reading. All of a sudden, the power went out and Marco decided to go to bed. Without the use of a flashlight or candle, Anna kept on reading. How?

Anna was blind. She was reading a book in Braille.

You move to an island in the middle of a lake. This lake is in a remote part of the state and there has never been a bridge connecting the island to the mainland. Every day a tractor and wagon gives rides around the island to tourists. Puzzled as to how the tractor had gotten onto the island, you ask around. You find out that the tractor was not built on the island and was not transported to the island by boat or by air. How did the tractor get to the island?

The owner waited until winter and then drove the tractor over on the frozen lake.

What is cut and spread out
on the table but never eaten?
A deck of cards.

A boy dreamed that a tiger was chasing him through the jungle. As the tiger got closer, the boy came to a tall tree. The boy quickly climbed to the top of the tree, but ran into a large python. Suddenly, he was in danger of being eaten by the snake and the tiger. How did he escape?

He woke up!

A woman cheered loudly for the winning soccer team's goalie. The woman is the goalie's sister, but the goalie is not the woman's brother. How are they related?

The goalie is the woman's sister.

One morning, a man is preparing to leave town, but first stops by his office to pick up his messages. While he is at the office, the night watchman stops him and says, "Sir, don't go on this trip. I had a dream last night that the plane will crash and you will die!" The man decides to cancel his trip. Just as the watchman predicted, the plane crashes and no one survives. The very next morning, the man rewards the watchman with one thousand dollars, but then fires him. Why would he fire the watchman who saved his life?

The "night" watchman was fired for sleeping on the job!

A man was found murdered on Sunday morning. His wife immediately notified the police. The police questioned the wife and staff and compiled these alibis:
The Wife said she was sleeping.
The Cook was cooking breakfast.
The Maid was gathering vegetables.
The Butler was getting the mail.
The police instantly arrested the murderer. Who did it and how did they know?

It was the Butler. He said he was getting the mail, but there is no mail on Sunday!

How can the statement "Four is half of five" be true?

If four is written in roman numerals (IV) then it is half of f(IV)E.

A woman shoots her husband. Then she holds him under water for over five minutes. Finally, she hangs him. But one hour later they both go out together and enjoy a wonderful dinner. How is this possible?

The woman was a photographer. She shot a picture of her husband, developed it, and hung it up to dry.

A murderer is condemned to death, but he is allowed to choose how he will be executed. The first choice is burnt at the stake, the second is shot by firing squad, and the third is given over to lions that haven't eaten in two years. Which choice is the best?

The third. Lions that haven't eaten in two years are dead.

What gets larger if you take anything away from it?

A hole.

What appears once in every minute,
twice in every moment, but not
once in a billion years?
The letter M.

Two men wearing packs are found on a mountain. One of the men is dead. The man who survived has his pack open, while the man who was killed has his pack closed. What was in the packs?

Parachutes. The dead man's chute didn't open.

Three men jumped off the Golden Gate Bridge, but one of them didn't get his hair wet. How is this possible?

He didn't have any hair.

Michael and Sophia have the same father and they were born at the same hour of the same day to the same mother in the same hospital. However, they are not twins. How is this possible?

They are two babies in a set of triplets.

A woman has seven children, half of them are boys. How can this be possible?

All the children are boys, so half are boys and so is the other half.

"I guarantee," said the salesman in the pet shop, "that this parrot will repeat every word it hears." A customer bought the bird, but found that the parrot wouldn't speak a single word. However, the salesman didn't lie about the bird. How is this possible?

The parrot was deaf.

What three-word sentence did Adam use when he met Eve for the first time? (Hint: It is read the same forwards and backwards!)

"Madam, I'm Adam."

Linda was making peach jam. She put all the peaches in the pot and began to cook them. Then she remembered she had to add one cup of sugar for every two peaches. How did she figure out how much sugar to add?

She counted the pits.

A horse is tied to a four-foot rope, and five feet away is a bale of hay. Without breaking the rope or chewing through it, the horse was able to get to the bale of hay. How is this possible?

The other end of the rope wasn't tied to anything.

If you were running a race, and you passed the person in second place, what place would you be in now?

You would be in second place.

Molly left a solid object on the kitchen counter while she went to play. When she came back four hours later, the object had completely vanished. No one touched it or ate it. What happened?

Molly left an ice cube on the counter.

Ancient Roman magicans used an ingenious method for walking through solid walls. What was it?
A door.

A boy was at a carnival and went to a booth where a man said to the boy, "If I write your exact weight on this piece of paper then you have to give me fifty dollars, but if I can't, I will pay you fifty dollars." The boy looked around and saw no scale so he agrees, thinking no matter what the man writes he'll just say he weighs more or less. In the end the boy ended up paying the man fifty dollars. How did the man win the bet?

The man did exactly as he said he would and wrote "your exact weight" on the paper.

Police found a man hanging in an empty room. There was nothing in the room he could have used to reach the ceiling. All they found when they entered the room was a puddle of water under the dead man. How did he hang himself?

He stood on a block of ice and let it melt.

Once upon a time, there was a clever thief charged with treason against the king and sentenced to die. However, the king decided to be a little merciful and let the thief choose which way he would die. Which way should he choose?

He should choose to die of old age.

A cowboy entered a Wild West bar and asked for a glass of water. The bartender drew a gun and pointed it at the young man. The young man said, "Thank you," and walked out. Why?

He had the hiccups and the bartender scared them out of him.

A man lives on the twenty-fifth floor of an apartment building. On rainy days, he takes the elevator to and from his apartment. However on sunny days, he will take the elevator from his apartment to the lobby, but walks up the twenty-five flights of stairs when he returns home. Why doesn't he just take the elevator all the time?

> *He's a very short man. On rainy days, he can hit the twenty-fifth button with his umbrella and of course he can always hit the lobby button because it's at the bottom of the console. On sunny days, he doesn't have any way of hitting the twenty-fifth button so he just takes the stairs.*

The ping-pong ball you are playing with drops into a long skinny hole in the floor. You can't stick your hand down the hole or use a tool to get it out. How can you get the ball without ripping out the floor?
Pour water down the hole. The ping-pong ball is light enough to float to the top!

Luke had it before, Paul had it behind. Ladies have it at the beginning. Abraham Lincoln had it twice. Doctor Lowell had it before and behind. He had it twice as bad behind as he did before. What was it?
> *The letter L.*

History & Geography

Why is Alabama the smartest
state in the United States?
  Because it has four A's and one B!

How did the colonists
react to the sugar tax?
  They raised cane.

What is the most slippery
country in the world?
  Greece.

Why did George Washington
sleep sitting up?
  Because he couldn't lie.

What bus sailed across
the Atlantic Ocean?
  Columbus.

What state of the United States
plays church music?
  Oregon.

How was the Roman
Empire cut in half?
With a pair of Caesars!

What state is always sick?
  Ill-inois.

What did Delaware do when Mississippi
lent Missouri her New Jersey?
  I don't know, Alaska.

What did Napoleon become
after his thirty-ninth birthday?
  Forty years old.

Why did Benjamin Franklin
like flying his kite?
He always got a charge out of it.

How did the Vikings
send secret messages?
By Norse code.

Where was the Declaration
of Independence signed?
At the bottom.

How much did the pirate pay
for his earrings?
A buccaneer.

Which U.S. President
liked to clean house?
Hoover.

What kind of knights
rode camels?
The Arabian knights.

Who invented King Arthur's
round table?
    Sir Cumference.

Where did the Pilgrims land
when they reached America?
    On their feet.

What state can you walk all over?
Floor-ida.

What are prehistoric monsters
called when they sleep?
    A dinosnore.

How did Columbus's men
sleep on their ships?
    With their eyes shut!

What is the fruitiest of
all school subjects?
    History, because it's full of dates!

Why were the early days of
history called the dark ages?
Because there were so many knights!

If April showers bring May
flowers, what do May flowers bring?
Pilgrims.

Why does the Statue of Liberty
stand in New York harbor?
Because she can't sit down!

What did Paul Revere say at
the end of his famous ride?
"Whoa!"

What did King George say when
he heard about the rebellious
American colonies?
"How revolting!"

What goes from Maine to Florida
without moving?
The highway.

What state is the cleanest?
Wash-ington.

What was Camelot?
*A place where people
parked their camels.*

Where was Solomon's temple?
Near his cheek.

What would you call theft in Peking?
A Chinese takeout!

Where is the biggest pencil
in the world?
Pencil-vania.

How can you name the capital of
every U.S. state in two seconds?
Say, "Washington, DC."

What country makes you shiver?
Chile.

What are the only two states that have
their state name in their state capital?
Oklahoma and Indiana.

Why were the Indians the
first people in North America?
They had reservations.

What rock group has four members,
all of whom are dead, one of
which was assassinated?
Mt. Rushmore.

Where do you find Timbuktu?
*Between Timbuk-one
and Timbuk-three.*

What did Mason say to Dixon?
"We have to draw the line."

What was the colonist's
favorite drink?
Liber-Tea.

What has four eyes
but can't see?
Mississippi.

What do you call people who
are always in a hurry?
Russians.

What country constantly has rain?
Bah-rain.

What did the flag say to
Thomas Jefferson?
Nothing. It just waved.

What do you call people who
like to travel a lot?
Romans.

What do history teachers talk
about when they get together?
The old days.

How were Martha Washington's
wigs delivered?
By hair mail.

When is a piece of wood
like Queen Elizabeth?
When the piece of wood is a ruler.

How is the United States similar
to a marathon runner?
They both have healthy constitutions.

What is the rope that
you never jump with?
Europe.

Which vegetable wasn't allowed
on Columbus's ships?
The leek.

What would happen if you threw
a white rock into the Black Sea?
It would get wet.

Where can you find roads without cars,
forests without trees, and cities without houses?
On a map.

If King Henry VIII were alive today,
what would he be most famous for?
Extreme old age.

What is found in the middle of America and Australia?
The letter R.

Before scientists traveled down the Nile River,
what was the longest river in the world?
The Nile River.

Human Nature

Where do you find a roof
that is always wet?
The roof of your mouth.

What belongs to you, but other people
use it more often?
Your name.

What part of your body is helpful
during the Boston Marathon?
A runny nose.

What does your friend have to
take before you can receive it?
Your photo.

What is the easiest
thing to part with?
A comb.

Who can marry many women
but still remain single?
A minister.

What cap is never removed?
Your knee cap.

How do you tell a lazy
man by his shoes?
See if he is wearing loafers.

What is the favorite color
of the human nose?
Blew.

What do you do to get
your eyes dressed up?
You clothes them.

What question can you
never answer with a yes?
"Are you sleeping?"

What boy likes to hang out
by the front door?
Matt.

What is the one thing you
can always count on?
Your fingers.

What part of the body is
the most popular?
*The tonsils, because they are
always being scheduled to come out.*

What did the rib cage say
to the heart and lungs?
"Got you covered!"

What joins two people but
only touches one?
A wedding ring.

When does your nose
smell the worst?
When it is stuffed up.

What do Christians take
when they have a cold?
Gos-pills.

How tall are you when
you do a handstand?
Two feet high.

What is over your head
and under your hat?
Your hair.

What part of your body
has the most rhythm?
Your eardrums.

What can you hold without
ever touching it?
A conversation.

In which month do people
exercise the least?
*February—it's the
shortest month.*

What are the most lucrative
teeth to leave for the tooth fairy?
Buck teeth.

The person sitting in the living room is
not your sibling but she is a child of your
mother and father.
Who is that person?
You.

When does your
lap disappear?
When you stand up.

What part of the human body
is most like a tree?
The palms.

Why was the fireman
lonely and sad?
He missed his old flame.

What do Eskimos get from
sitting on the ice too long?
Polaroids.

Why are talkative people
generally overweight?
They like to chew the fat.

What office job do fingernails
dislike the most?
Filing.

How do chess players tell fairy tales?
"Once a-pawn a time. . ."

What can you say about
a girl named Sugar?
She is probably refined.

Where do twins
usually sleep?
In double beds.

What boy is always around
to fix your flat tire?
Jack.

What kind of animals
do most people own?
Calves.

What do you leave behind only after you take one?
A footstep.

What is the one thing that every human
being has had except for Adam and Eve?
Parents.

What walks on four legs in the morning,
two legs in the afternoon, and three legs
in the evening? (Riddle of the Sphinx.)
*A man—crawls as a baby, walks as an adult,
and uses a cane when elderly.*

Why did the wandering traveler
burn down her house?
She loved home cooking.

What counts up but
never counts down?
Your age.

What did Sarah try to use to replace her lost tooth?
Toothpaste.

What is the best way to avoid
hitting your fingers with a hammer?
Hold the hammer with both hands.

What do you call a girl who
always has change?
Penny.

Can you name something that you get to keep even
when you give it to someone?
Your word.

What do you call an aunt who
runs off to get married?
An antelope.

What is the best way to
eliminate wrinkles?
With an iron.

What should you do if
your ears are ringing?
Answer them.

What do people make
that you can't see?
Noise.

Why did the two hairs
say farewell?
*They knew parting was
such sweet sorrow.*

What is a good
name for lawyers?
Sue.

What is a good name
for a thief?
Rob.

If Bob's father is Ben's son,
what relation is Bob to Ben?
Ben is Bob's grandfather.

How can Sarah physically stand
behind Kate if Kate is physically
standing behind Sarah?
The two girls are standing back to back.

What gets darker as the
room becomes lighter?
Your shadow.

What do opticians call
their annual dance?
The eye ball.

Why did the aging
climber quit hiking?
He was already over the hill.

What can you catch but not hold?
  A cold.

What is the oldest part of a man's body?
    *The Adam's apple. It has
    been there since the beginning.*

In the Kitchen

What is the best way to
keep food bills down?
With a paperweight!

How can you tell the difference between a
can of chicken soup and a can of turkey soup?
Read the label.

What did the mayonnaise
say to the refrigerator?
"Close the door! I'm dressing."

What kind of soda is
dangerous to drink?
Baking soda.

What kind of food will
you find in heaven?
Angel food cake.

Why was the ketchup
last in the race?
It couldn't catch up.

What has four legs, a head, and leaves?
A dining room table.

What did the hot dog say
when he won the race?
"I'm the wiener."

When do you find
pickles at the door?
When it is ajar.

What did the chef say
to the Caesar salad?
*"You are big enough to
get dressed yourself."*

What's green and bores holes?
A drill pickle.

What do you call an apple
with a short temper?
A crab apple.

What food can you catch a virus from?
Wheat germ.

Why did the cabbage win the race?
It was a-head!

What kind of nut comes without a shell?
A doughnut.

What did the banana
say to the orange?
I'm peeling so loved!

What is most useful when
it has been broken?
An egg.

How did Ms. Melon refuse
the marriage proposal?
"Because I cant-aloupe!"

How do you know if
a chef is in trouble?
See if his goose is cooked.

What rises every morning
but is not the sun?
The bread in a bakery.

Where do hot dogs dance?
At meat balls.

What book has the
most stirring topics?
A cookbook.

What is black when you buy it,
red when you use it, and gray
when you throw it away?
Charcoal.

Why shouldn't you tell
secrets around produce?
*The corn has ears, the potatoes
have eyes, and the beanstalk.*

What can be peeled and chipped,
but will never crack?
A potato.

What dessert comes in
an edible container?
An ice-cream cone.

What soup is good
for your brain?
Noodle soup.

Where did the cup and
saucer go for vacations?
To China.

Why did the hot dog
wear a sweater?
Because it was a chili dog.

How did Sally flatter
the potato?
She buttered it up.

Why did the sub sandwich
get a medal?
Because he was a hero.

What is the smallest room in the world?
A mushroom.

What did the vegetables say
after getting stuck in the fridge?
"Lettuce out!"

Which of these fruits does not belong:
apple, peach, banana,
strawberry, pear?
*The banana. It's the only one that
needs to be peeled before eating.*

What kind of drink will give
you a black-and-blue face?
Punch.

What lives in the ground and has eyes,
but doesn't have a mouth or nose?
A potato.

Name two things you
can't have for breakfast.
Lunch and dinner.

What kind of apple
isn't an apple?
A pineapple.

Why is the cookie so bitter?
It has a chip on its shoulder.

What did the zombie always
put on his mashed potatoes?
Grave-y.

What fruits are most often
mentioned in history?
Dates.

Why was the chef arrested?
*He was caught beating the
eggs and whipping the cream.*

What do you always find
asleep in the dining room?
Napkins.

What kind of coffee
do you drink on the train?
Expresso.

What always stays hot
even in the refrigerator?
Salsa.

What vegetable has the best rhythm?
Beets.

What kind of cheese did
Frankenstein like?
  Muenster.

What cereal always puts
a smile on your face?
  Grinola.

What looks just
like half an apple?
  The other half.

What fruit goes well
with any drink?
  Strawberries.

What kind of cup has
trouble holding water?
  A cupcake.

How do you know when
the grapes are old and tired?
  They start to wine.

What is the best way to
make meatloaf?
Send your cow on vacation.

What fruit is often
hired by the Navy?
Naval oranges.

Why won't you ever
find a lonely banana?
Because they always stay in bunches.

How do salad dressings
like to sleep?
On a bed of lettuce.

What kind of jam
can't you eat?
A traffic jam.

Why wasn't the girl hurt when
she fell into a puddle of Coke?
Because it was a soft drink.

Odds & Ends

How many three-cent
stamps are in a dozen?
There are twelve three-cent stamps in a dozen.

When does saying
something's name kill it?
Silence.

What is purchased by the
yard and used by the foot?
Carpet.

What is big when it is new but
gets smaller with each use?
A bar of soap.

What goes up and down
but doesn't move?
  A staircase.

What is the saddest
time of the day?
  Mourning.

What would you get if seven
hundred stamps were running
one hundred miles per hour?
  A stampede.

What consumes itself and dies
as soon as it is devoured?
  A candle.

What three things have eyes
but cannot see?
  Needles, potatoes, and hurricanes.

What kind of clothing
do cities wear?
  Outskirts.

What can run but can't walk?
Water.

What goes around the yard but never moves?
A fence.

What did the cold computer say to the camp fire? "Log on."

What has wheels and flies?
A garbage truck.

What has four legs
but only one foot?
A bed.

Where did the city store its taxis?
In a cab-inet.

Why did the hikers find
Mt. Washington so funny?
It was hill-arious.

What points up when it's light but
points down when it is dark?
 A light switch.

Which is heavier, a pound of
feathers or a pound of bricks?
 *Neither. Both groups weigh
exactly one pound.*

What color is
always screaming?
Yell-ow!

What musical instrument
has the best character?
 The upright piano.

What makes a chess
player happy?
Taking the knight off.

What has a head and a tail,
is brown, but has no legs?
 A penny.

What can you draw
without a pencil or paper?
A window shade.

What musical instrument do
computers like to play?
The keyboard.

What goes up when the rain
begins to come down?
Your umbrella.

What did one elevator say
to the other elevator?
"I am coming down with something."

What goes all over the world
yet stays in a corner?
A stamp.

How many sides does
a circle have?
Two. The inside and the outside.

What can run but will not walk,
has a mouth but will not talk,
has a bed but will not sleep?
   A river.

What did one wall
say to the other?
"Meet me in the corner."

What is the first sign that
your computer is getting old?
Memory loss.

What would be worse than
finding a worm in your apple?
   Finding half a worm in your apple!

What did the rug say to the floor?
"Don't move; I've got you covered."

Which two words contain
the most letters?
   Post office.

What did one magnet
say to the other?
"I find you very attractive."

What is the best day
to go to the beach?
Sun-day.

What can fly when it is on
and float when it is off?
A feather.

Why was the computer
declared a hero?
He was always saving things.

What did the necktie
say to the hat?
*"You go on ahead. I'll hang
around for a while."*

How did the fireplace feel?
Grate!

Who can jump higher than a house?
Anyone. A house can't jump.

What building has
the most stories?
A library!

How did the rain
make the ghost upset?
It dampened her spirits.

What did the window
say to the nurse?
"I have this pane."

What is easy to return
but impossible to borrow?
Gratitude.

What has fifty
heads and fifty tails?
A roll of pennies.

What asks no question but
demands an answer?
   The doorbell.

In what language do baked
goods communicate?
   Danish.

What has a fork and mouth, but never eats food?
A river.

What kind of soap
do telephones use?
   Dial.

Did you hear about the two
telephones that got married?
   It was a double-ring ceremony.

What never was,
but always will be?
   Tomorrow.

What is the best thing to
take into the desert?
A thirst-aid kit.

What has three legs when resting
but only one leg when working?
A wheelbarrow.

Where do you find good
sandwiches in India?
Try New Delhi.

Why wouldn't Silly Sam
walk barefoot in the grass?
Because it was full of blades.

Which months of the year
have twenty-eight days?
All of them.

What time is it when a
clock strikes thirteen?
Time to get a new clock.

What kind of lights did
Noah have on the ark?
Floodlights.

What did the clock's big hand
say to the little hand?
"I'll see you in an hour."

What moves around all day and
sits in your room at night with
its tongue hanging out?
A shoe.

What never gets sick but is always
broken out with twenty-one spots?
A six-sided die.

What kind of paper
makes you itch?
Scratch paper.

Do you say "eight and four is eleven"
or "eight and four are eleven"?
Neither. Eight and four is twelve.

What is strong enough to hold
a stone but can't hold water?
A sieve.

How did Igor know where
to find Frankenstein?
He had a hunch.

What are the strongest
days of the week?
*Saturday and Sunday. All other
days are weak (week) days!*

What is the only thing left
after a train goes by?
Its tracks.

Who was the best actor
in the Bible?
*Samson. He brought
the house down!*

What is the favorite mode of
transportation for accountants?
Tax-is.

What did the mother book say to
her son before he left for the playground?
"Don't lose your jacket!"

What day of the week is
named after a number?
Two's day.

What holds water
but is full of holes?
A sponge.

What do you call the
science of shopping?
Buy-ology.

What season do skydivers
love the best?
Fall.

What can you feed and it will grow,
but give it water and it will die?
Fire.

What does Payless Shoes call its
annual holiday party?
The foot ball.

What has nothing left but a nose
after you remove its eye?
Noise.

What Am I?

I am cracked; I am made.
I am told; I am played.
What am I?
   A joke.

I have four legs, two sides, one foot, and
one head. Cozy and comfy when covered
with a spread. What am I?
   A bed.

When full, I can point the way,
but when empty, nothing moves me.
I have two skins—one outside and
one inside. What am I?
   A glove.

I am the ruler of shovels.
I have a double.
I am as thin as a knife.
I have a wife.
What am I?
   *The King of Spades from
   a deck of cards.*

I am as round as the moon, the color
of fine silver, and the hole in my
middle helps me to play.
What am I?
A compact disc.

The higher I climb, the hotter I become.
My crystal cage is always my home.
What am I?
Mercury in a thermometer.

I have three hands
that rotate regularly around and
around; my second hand is really last,
and usually makes a sound.
What am I?
   A clock with a second hand.

Dark with white writing,
and smooth like a slate.
Teachers depend on me,
and students clean my face.
What am I?
  A chalkboard or blackboard.

Thousands hoard gold in this house,
but no human built it. Spears are busy
keeping watch, but no human guards it.
What is it?
  A beehive.

They call me a man, but I'll never have a life.
I was given a body, but will never have a wife.
They made me a mouth, but I cannot sing.
Water gives me life and death comes in spring.
What am I?
  A snowman.

What force and strength cannot break
through, I with barely a touch can do.
And many in the street would wait,
Were I not a friend to the gate.
What am I?
  A key.

I come in different shapes and sizes. Part
of me has curves; part of me is straight.
You can put me anywhere you like,
but there is only one right place for me.
What am I?
   A jigsaw puzzle piece.

My life is often a container of woe,
my leaves require assistance to turn just
so. Hard is my spine and my insides are
pale, yet I'm always ready to tell a good
tale. What am I?
A book.

I can speak every language ever known
to man, but I have never attended school
and I tend to bounce around.
What am I?
   An echo.

Bright as diamonds; loud as thunder;
never still; a thing of wonder.
What am I?
Fireworks.

I am used to bat with, yet
I never get a hit. I am near a
ball, yet it is never thrown.
What am I?
 Eyelashes.

Fire is often lit above me, and if
you delete my first letter, you will
find where everyone you have
ever known was born.
What am I?
The hearth.

I can be an excellent seamstress,
but my eye can't see a stitch that I sew.
What am I?
A needle.

Though fluid at birth,
don't shove me too far.
Beware if I break,
for the outcome may scar.
What am I?
 Glass.

Part carbon and part water,
but I am poison to fishes.
Many falsely claim my name,
I am the pause that refreshes.
What am I?
A soda.

I am cold as steel, but made of flesh.
Never thirsty, but I surround
myself with liquid.
What am I?
A fish.

I always tell the truth, and reflect
everything I see. You'll find me in
all shapes and sizes. What could I be?
A mirror.

I cannot be felt, seen, or touched; yet
I can be found in everyone.
My existence is always in debate;
yet I have my own style of music.
What am I?
A soul.

Once upon a time, there was a green house.
Inside the green house, there were white walls.
Inside the white walls, there was red furniture.
Living in the house were lots of babies.
What is it?

> *A watermelon.*

My life can be measured in hours, and I
serve by being devoured.
If thin, I am quick; if fat, I am slow.
I must always beware that wind is my foe.
What am I?

> *A candle.*

You hope you never have it. But when
you do, you hope you never lose it.
What is it?

> *A lawsuit.*

I am the briefest complete
sentence in the English language.
What am I?

> *I am! (Complete sentences always
> require a noun and verb. Imperative
> commands do not count.)*

I never was, but will always be. As soon as
I arrive, then I am gone. Everyone depends
on me, but they don't always look
forward to me.
What am I?
    Tomorrow.

At night they come without being called
and move around without being walled.
But at the very first sign of light,
they disappear back into the night.
What are they?
Stars.

Around three o'clock, I often bathe.
I like my water hot.
A part of me just seeps away,
and then I hit the spot.
What am I?
A tea bag.

I am taken from a mine, and shut up
in a wooden case from which I am
never released. Yet, I am used by
almost everyone.
What am I?
    Pencil lead.

Not an airplane, but I can float across the sky.
Not a river, but full of water am I.
What am I?
 A cloud.

Only one color, but many a size,
stuck on the bottom, yet easily flies.
Present in sun, but never in rain,
doing no harm, and feeling no pain.
What am I?
 Your shadow!

I can be pronounced as one letter,
but I am written with three.
Read from both ends, and
I am steady as a tree.
What am I?
 The word eye.

I can be cool, but I am never cold.
I can be sorry, but I won't be guilty.
I can be spooked, but I can't be anxious.
I can be sweet, but I don't include candy.
I can be swallowed, but I will never be eaten.
What am I?
 Words with double letters.

I can be published, I can be spoken,
I can be uncovered, I can be broken.
What am I?
   News.

The beginning of eternity;
the end of time and space.
The beginning of every end,
and the end of every place.
What am I?
   The letter E.

With pointed teeth I sit and wait,
to join my victims and determine fate.
My bloodless subjects show no fright,
even when I pounce for a single bite.
What am I?
   A stapler.

You can hear me calling,
summoning with a bell;
you never know if I
want to greet or sell.
What am I?
  A telephone.

I have many legs, but need assistance
to stand. I have a long neck, but no
head or eyes to see. I keep things clean,
but I am usually quite dirty.
What am I?
  A broom.

What Do You Get?

What do you get if you cross
a garden hose and an elephant?
A jumbo jet.

What do you get if you cross
a snowman with a crocodile?
Frostbite!

What do you get when you
cross a blanket with butter?
A bed spread.

What do you get if you cross
a goose with Dracula?
  A count down.

What do you get if you cross
a chicken and an earthquake?
  A bunch of scrambled eggs.

What do you get when you
buy a boat at discount?
A sale boat.

What do you get if you cross
a watermelon and a school bus?
  *A watermelon with
  forty-five seeds (seats).*

What do you get if you cross a
skunk and a boomerang?
A smell that always comes back.

What do you get if you cross
Glenn Miller with dynamite?
A blast from the past.

What do you get when you have
a cross between "star" and "led"?
Star-t-led.

What do you get if you cross
a cow and an octopus?
A cow that can milk itself.

What do you get if you cross a
groundhog and a tardy student?
Six more weeks of detention.

What do you get when you
put three ducks in a box?
A box of quackers.

What do you get when you cross
a parrot with a centipede?
A walkie-talkie!

What do you get if you
cross a kangaroo and an iguana?
Leaping lizards.

What do you get when you cross
steak knives and two rolling pins?
A set of roller-blades.

What do you get if you cross
a nun and a chicken?
A pecking order!

What do you get when you
practice kung fu in the forest?
Chopsticks.

What do you get when you cross
a pony express horse and a kangaroo?
A horse with a built-in mail pouch.

What do you get when you
drop a letter in a mud puddle?
Blackmail.

What do you get if you cross
a boomerang with a Chia Pet?
A present that returns itself.

What do you get when you cross
a computer and a mosquito?
Too many bytes.

What do you get if you cross
a novel and a vampire?
*A book that you can
really sink your teeth into.*

What do you get when you
cross a big cat and a weed?
   A dandy lion.

What do you get when you
cross a rooster and a wolf?
*An animal that howls
when the sun rises.*

What do you get when you
cross a mummy with a beggar?
A bum wrap.

What do you get when you
cross a reptile with a side street?
   An alley-gator.

What do you get when you cross
a bird, a car, and a dog?
A flying carpet.

What Is the Difference?

What is the difference between a
sharpshooter and a refreshing drink?
*One hits the target and
the other hits the spot.*

What's the difference between
a mirror and a gossip?
*One reflects without talking
and one talks without reflecting.*

What is the difference between a
student and a farmer tending his cows?
*One is stocking his mind for life,
while the other is minding his livestock.*

What is the difference
between a bird and a fly?
A bird can fly, but a fly can't bird.

What's the difference between
a pear and a pearl?
The letter L.

What is the difference between
a December morning
and a bad boxer?
*One is cold out and
the other is out cold.*

What is the difference
between here and there?
The letter T.

What is the difference between
a shiny penny and a dirty nickel?
Four cents.

What is the difference between
the planet Earth and her oceans?
Earth is dirt-y and the oceans are tide-y.

What's the difference between a
counterfeit dollar bill and a crazy rabbit?
*One is bad money; the
other is a mad bunny!*

What is the difference between
diapers and ten-dollar bills?
One is easier to change than the other.

What is the difference between
a gardener and a dry cleaner?
*One keeps the lawn moist and
the other the laun-dry.*